CREDO?

CREDO?
Religion and Psychoanalysis

Patrick Casement

AEON

Aeon Books Ltd
12 New College Parade
Finchley Road
London NW3 5EP

British Library Cataloguing in Publication Data

A C.I.P. for this book is available from the British Library

ISBN-13: 978-1-91280-763-5

Typeset by Medlar Publishing Solutions Pvt Ltd, India

Printed in Great Britain

www.aeonbooks.co.uk

Namaste

May the sacred in me recognise
and salute the sacred in you

To Arthur

CONTENTS

ACKNOWLEDGEMENTS

I am principally indebted to our grandson, Arthur Wakes-Miller, who first encouraged me to put together this further selection of my writings, those prompted by my interest in the parallels between religion and psychoanalysis.

I owe much to Robert Mitchell who, as chaplain in the Royal Free Hospital, London, embodied the potency of listening during my five months there. It was throughout those many hours that I came to revisit what I am sharing here.

I have felt especially supported by Father Bob Hanson and his similar distrust of sureness. He has also gently guided me towards greater tact in some of my more critical comments.

I owe a great deal to my colleague and friend, Beni Woolmer, for her persistent belief that I should offer more widely the thoughts I have put together here.

Once again, I am grateful to Dr Patricia Morris for her incisive editing and her enthusiastic encouragement throughout. She also helped me to benefit from the skills of Monica Franco who designed the front cover. I also wish to express my thanks to David Black,[1] for contributing a Foreword to this book, and to Rowan Williams for his Commendation.

---

[1] David M Black, psychoanalyst and author of *Psyhoanalysis and Religion in the 21st Century*.

As ever, in the background, I have always been supported by my wife: the *sine qua non* behind all I have done and in my writing.

Permissions have been granted for the more recent publications. The early publications may be beyond obtaining permission.

COMMENDATION

Dr Rowan Williams

Philosophers, religious apologists, sociologists and psychologists, advertisers and politicians are all in their different ways interested in what makes us sure of our choices and our perceptions; and we are encouraged to think well of those who show no sign of unsureness. Sometimes there is a moral charge to this as well: not to be sure is somehow to refuse a challenge, to commitment or clarity or whatever; to stick selfishly to a detached stance that keeps options open.

One of the great contributions of this moving book is the way in which it helps us question this set of assumptions. Patrick Casement is very far from recommending a lazy and uncommitted 'open-mindedness'. On the contrary, he uses his insight as an analyst to focus on the ways in which easy certainties set up a barrier against the full demands of difficult truths, the ways in which they teach us to live in a smaller world than we need for our health and sanity. He writes powerfully about the very different kind of 'sureness' that is given by the sheer fact of another person's commitment to listen and be present, and about the profound respect for one another that recognises what it is in the other that can never be known.

In a way, as this book gently reminds us time after time, you can see religious belief and practice as always poised between these two kinds of certainty, repeatedly tempted by (and succumbing to) the lure of rapid and decisive sureness, yet unable to shake off its own heritage of wondering and faithful not-knowing, as it turns towards an unknown source of light. 'Non-certainty', says Casement, 'does not have to be a defence against ignorance ... It takes the confidence of experience for an analyst to be able to maintain non-certainty as the creative mind-set it can be.' That difficult but life-giving place of confidence is also where durable and mature belief belongs, a deep trust that is not about the sureness of a scheme or a picture but about the knowledge of being listened to and held in attention. Learning to stand in that elusive spot is the key to learning something about a *living* not a *passive* truth. That insight is at the heart of these searching pages, and it is a vital one.

FOREWORD FOR *CREDO?*

Patrick Casement's title makes two crucial points with impressive economy. The external world comes, to a large extent, already divided up into the units that have to be named: every language is bound to have words meaning *dog*, and *tree*, and *bicycle*. But the inner world, the world of subjective experience, is indistinct: it isn't clear what has to be named, and its realities are to some extent brought into being, and given structure, only when words are put to them. That is why religions are different from one another, and it's also why psychoanalysis never quite settles down, and is always generating new theory.

So, in Casement's title, both the *credo* and the question mark are doing important work. To discover and develop the inner world, we have to take the risk of giving credence to some vocabulary or other—"believing"—but if we fail to question that vocabulary we will be taken in by it—will "believe in it" in the rigid sense that has given belief a bad name in the minds of so many intelligent people today.

In this book, Patrick Casement looks back over the history of his own relationship with Christian belief. Casement is well known in psychoanalytic circles for writing with remarkable simplicity about very delicate matters, particularly moments in therapy when the analyst "learns from the patient" and has to deepen or alter his or her initial beliefs or perceptions. Such moments replace the picture of the all-knowing analyst with the idea of someone not expert, but continually interrogating his or her understanding in the light of an ever-new situation. In a similar way, the present book celebrates "non-certainty" in religion.

It takes courage to write undefendedly about the reality of what happens between patient and analyst, and that courage is evident in this book too. Casement looks back over a lifelong relationship to Christianity. He started out as a devout theology student, perhaps on a path to being ordained as a priest, and was then horribly disillusioned by the Church's insensitive response to a painful life-crisis. He includes several of his early publications from the 1960s, so that we meet very directly the earnest, passionate, angry and very intelligent young man he was at that time, and then the larger part of the book consists of his more developed reflections from the 1990s onward. In a fine discussion of the Grand Inquisitor's harangue in Dostoyevski's *The Brothers Karamazov*, he gives us a beautiful account of the difference between rigid religious belief and the spontaneous recognition of emotional truth—of the harshness and deadness of the *credo* when it forgets its question mark.

This openness of attitude allows him too to mine the metaphorical resources of the Christian story (without needing to imply that it is *only* a metaphor). He speaks of the "Resurrection principle", that new life can grow out of death, as present in the consulting room, and I admire especially his emphasis on the importance of the analyst being willing to stay with the patient's suffering "for as long as it takes", without retreating into knowingness or optimism. This is an attitude that requires "faith" (in a certain sense) of the analyst. Having worked with patients whose analysts had been unable to do this, I resonated with this idea in particular.

Psychoanalysis has not, in general, been at ease in allowing religion any importance in its own right. Starting with Freud, it "knew better". But this has changed increasingly over the years. And, of course, the more responsible religions are changing also. Patrick Casement's attractive and serious book is a valuable contribution to a continuing development.

David M. Black

PREFACE

In this collection of writings, put together over sixty years, I am trying to share something of my own search for a meaning in life.

My quest eventually became a conversation between religion and psychoanalysis, noticing similarities between them and what each could learn from the other.

I record here some of what I encountered within my own idiom. I am not assuming that any of it need apply to others beyond what they may relate to themselves. Ultimately, I believe that truth for each is what *feels true* to each.

INTRODUCTION

This mini-book was never meant to happen. I had determined that my recent publication *Learning along the Way* would be my last book on psychoanalysis, and so it is. But this 'book' is different. It is only a mini-book, a 'booklet', and it is about a different range of interests.

The early writings here come from a side of my life that has been much less known, different from what I had most often been writing about.

I have put together here some recent thoughts and wonderings, along with earlier writings that were published way back when I was preoccupied with theology and still thinking that I might offer myself for ordination.

As in all my writing, I am asking questions that I believe need to be asked, whether or not they can really be answered. Often, however, we may be reaching for answers in order to deflect the discomfort caused by difficult questions we might prefer to silence.

My approach here has been to question all belief rather than just accepting it. That is why my main title here is *Credo?*

I also question any belief system that has been adopted in the name of orthodoxy, or out of loyalty to group thinking that tends to form around whatever positions of theory are adhered to.

Many questions

I have always been asking questions: how do things work, why is the world as it is, where do we fit into the cosmos we find ourselves in? What is 'truth'?

Does life have to be dull, seeming to be pointless, dark and depressing? At times it can seem so, especially when walking with eyes staring down at one's feet. But does it always have to be like that?

When I raise my eyes I can be lifted to the skies, to the tops of mountains, to the sights and sounds of nature in all its magnificence, and I can then become more aware of all that I see and hear around me.

How could such beauty have come about, in flowers and birds, the amazing variety of animals, fishes and insects, along with the extraordinary interrelatedness of so many different species? Has all of this just happened as a result of billions of years of evolution?

Also, how was it I could be moved to tears by something as beautiful and utterly perfect as Michelangelo's *Pieta*, in St Peter's, Rome? And, later, to find myself inconsolable when some crazed idiot chose to attack that most perfect of all pieces of sculpture, destroying its sublime perfection forever?

And how is it that I can be so moved by a painting such as "The girl with a pearl earring" by Vermeer? Or be lifted up by music, as with that duo of trumpet and voice in Handel's "Eternal Source of Light Divine", as sung by Elin Manahan Thomas. (I really want that at my funeral.)

What is it that lies beyond our knowing, beyond our imagination and beyond our understanding: beyond the reach of either science or philosophy?

Might there be some unimaginable energy, some incomprehensible wisdom and purpose, that will forever remain beyond our comprehending?

Might the very idea of God be our own invention? As Voltaire famously said: "If there were not a God we'd need to invent one."

So, behind and beyond the heady business of Church debate, and the rituals we witness in some churches we may visit or attend, what might be the ultimate truth to which all of this may claim to bear witness?

But, whenever we look at liturgical presentations of what that man Jesus is said to have stood for, what do we find?

Are we lifted up? Are we moved to consider a sense of transcendence, and are we touched by the essential message Jesus is said to have represented before that teaching became institutionalised?

Are we inspired to look upon the image of crucified love; a love we are told was given for all people of all times, even if we cannot comprehend that? Might it inspire us to find also in ourselves a capacity for that selfless giving for others, and perhaps a capacity for forgiveness of others? And might we consider walking alongside that said-to-be divine figure, whose example and teaching has been affecting the world over the past two thousand years, even though that influence has too often been more destructive than admirable?

Or are we inclined to turn away from all of that, thinking it might be merely a creation of our own wish to find some purpose in a world that can so readily seem to be without sense or meaning?

And when we are most inclined to dismiss religion, might we simply be recalling the oft referred to notion of Karl Marx that religion could merely be "the opium of the people"?

Also, we do not have to look far to find, as I shall be recalling below, what we can claim as reasons for turning our backs upon religion so that we can remain untroubled by any idea of still 'believing' in anything to do with religion.

* * *

The following reflections, partly meditative, were written to clarify my own thinking.

I know there is an extensive literature on religion and psychoanalysis, but I do not here engage with any of it. My own questioning has been mostly private and I did not want to be diverted by books. That was never going to be my way.

Instead, I have simply indicated some of the steps along my own journey, initially engaging with ideas that were current in Cambridge while I was there between 1956 and 1959.

I wrote the brief article "A False Security?" in 1960, with no thought of publication. It was only in the wake of John Robinson's *Honest to God* (1963) that I explored the possibility that this might be considered for publication, which it was in 1964. Strangely, I had never read Robinson's book until I had finished putting together this present collection of writings. I sensed that I would probably know already what he was saying, which to some extent I did.

This collection is therefore offered to the reader in the hope that some of it might resonate in the minds of others who have been asking similar questions about life, and why are we here.

CHAPTER ONE

Objections to Christian religion

The message or the messenger?

One of the most telling reasons for rejecting the message of Christianity can be found in the lives of the 'messengers,' who are there to represent the gospel they claim to be preaching.

What connection, if any, can there be between the pomp and show, which we see in many churches, and the simple life of that carpenter's son, Jesus?

Too often we see priests caught up in the trappings of their own glory, their own egos sometimes shining more noticeably than does the life and death of the man they preach about and point towards.

Our attention can be diverted by what often looks like self-promotion amongst those who claim to have been called to serve God and others.

The Church, sin and sex

Throughout the ages, we can see that the Christian Church has never sorted out how to view sex, other than to regard it mostly as sinful and dangerous: as *original sin*.

What seems to have been lost sight of is that every society has aimed to contain whatever could threaten its stability, most often using religion as a way of social control—for the sake of social harmony and cohesion.

Attempts at guarding the family unit

Religion has oft been used to protect the family, especially when there was no reliable contraception. Religious laws were drawn up, aiming to avoid pregnancy outside an established relationship, in order to protect and nurture any child that might be conceived. For those who disregarded those laws of relationship there were often penalties—both social and 'religious'. The aim was basically to control and protect the communal life, but mostly that control was by fear.

In modern times the developments in contraception, and changes in social norms, have inevitably led to a new freedom. But this has not always been a social gain. We have now found a freedom that is often chaotic, especially in the realms of sexuality and family.

Sex and the Church

There has been a parallel disintegration in the Church too, with regard to sex and sexuality. In particular there seems to have been a serious split between established claims of sexual abstinence, as with vows of celibacy and/or chastity, especially amongst the clergy and those monks who take such vows. The public *persona* of those 'ministers of the gospel' often seems to have become a mask behind which much else may lie hidden.

Different extremes

I was shocked by the extremes I encountered when I most needed to find support and understanding from those who were there to represent the God they claimed to serve. In fact I was so shocked I turned my back, for many years, on church-going of any kind.

I then refused to have anything to do with the Church that I had seen so badly represented by what I regarded as hypocrisy, on the one hand, and by an extraordinary and insane detachment on the other.

Two examples

In 1961, when my life was collapsing in crisis, I sought solace from two 'ministers' of the Church at a particular time of personal anguish. (See chapter 2 in my book *Learning from Life*, 2006.)

The extremely different responses I got from those two people led me to reject Christianity altogether, at least as represented by those said-to-be 'holy' men.

The person I had hoped to marry, Janet, had chosen instead to marry my former friend David. I had also learned that Janet was in the process of dying. She had Hodgkin's lymphoma, which in those days was incurable. (Fortunately the treatment of this has been much improved since then.)

Whilst I was still reeling from the shock of all that ('on rebound' from losing Janet) I found myself in a relationship with a lovely person called Helen. But I soon realised she was becoming much more deeply attached to me than I could ever be to her.

Once I realised this I resolved to end my relationship with her. But Helen wouldn't have that, and she set about persuading me I hadn't *really* come to break off our relationship. Instead, she said I had really come to ask her to marry me, claiming I had "just lacked the courage to say that."

What followed was a disaster. We became 'engaged.' Helen then came to meet my family, as my fiancée, and they liked her. But I became increasingly depressed that I had involved her in something I could never see through. I therefore *had* to break off the engagement.

I knew this had hurt Helen: *seriously* hurt her. And, knowing this also caused me deep distress. Of course I felt a profound sense of guilt, which I was totally unable to deal with. So I looked for help.

Seeking help

It so happened that a certain Brother 'P,' of the Society of St Francis (SSF), was then staying at my Oxford college, Christ Church. I had come to know him through my own association with those Franciscan friars. In fact I had earlier been enrolled as a lay associate of their society.

I had believed that Brother 'P' might be able to understand something of my concern for Helen, knowing that I had so deeply hurt her. When I went to speak with him, at first it seemed as if he did.

Near the end of my time with him he said he regretted he had not yet been ordained, else he would have heard my confession. That at least might help to allay my sense of guilt. He therefore recommended I went to see Father 'T.' This was none other than the Very Revd Professor 'T,' a prominent and well-known cleric, who happened to be resident in Christ Church at the time. I agreed to do this.

But then something terrible happened. Brother 'P' tried to *grope* me, and gestured that he wanted me to grope him in return.

I was utterly shocked. Where was this friar's empathy for me and for Helen? Where was his pastoral care for those in distress? And what about his vow of chastity? What was this about? How did this fit with his 'holy' calling? It clearly didn't. He was just in search of some gratification for himself.

4

I turned away from Brother 'P' utterly shocked. I just said to him, before leaving: "You must be very lonely." There was no reply.

A second attempt at getting help

I next went to see Father 'T,' as it had been suggested it might help if I made my confession. "Might help" indeed!

I tried to convey to Father 'T' my distress about Helen, that I had so deeply hurt her and could not think how I could do anything to lessen her pain, except to reinstate our engagement which I knew I could not do.

After telling all I could of what was distressing me, Father 'T' proceeded to demonstrate how utterly cut off from life he was.

All he could say was to ask me if I had committed "*the sin of fornication*." I wasn't even sure what counted as *fornication*, and what did not. I knew I hadn't had intercourse, but I had no idea how to describe the intimacy I'd actually had with Helen. Was it 'fornication' or not? I didn't know. And why did it matter?[2]

Father 'T' told me he could not give me absolution from my sins unless I told him if I had committed the 'sin' of fornication. To this I replied: "I have no idea if I had, or had not, *fornicated*. But, let's say I had."

Father 'T' went through the ritual of giving me absolution, and setting a penance—that I should read through a particular psalm he prescribed for me. He then withdrew to pray for me.

During the ensuing silence I thought deeply on that ghastly sequence, from Brother 'P' to Father 'T,' and I made a sudden

---

[2] It has since been pointed out to me that I should not be putting all the blame onto that particular cleric for the insensitivity he was demonstrating. Apparently, at that time, he would have been *required* by the Church to have all sins explicitly specified before granting absolution. How absurd!

decision. I was not going to have anything further to do with a Church that was represented by such absurd 'ministers' as these.

I went back to this well-known cleric and said to him: "I have considered all of this very carefully and I have come to a decision. *You can stuff your so-called absolution up your own backside*! I am turning my back on all of this superficial nonsense, maybe forever. *Goodbye*."

I happened to bump into that cleric several years later, on a pedestrian crossing by Sloane Square, and I told him that I had never forgotten, nor had I forgiven, his crass handling of my attempt to find some help at a time when I had been in crisis.

I added that I was then training to be a psychotherapist and I hoped I might become more helpful to people in distress than he had been for me. I confirmed that I had continued to turn my back on all that he stood for. And I added: "I still don't know what counts as *fornication* and what doesn't!" Of course there was no reply he could make to this.

Since then much has changed: see later.

CHAPTER TWO

The cup of Baptism

Is Baptism little more than a naming-event, or may it potentially point to something much more profound?

This came to me while I was living 'in community' with Canon Roland Walls, 1960, during my time with the Industrial Mission in Sheffield along with five ordinands. We spent six months working in industry followed by five months living together under the pastoral leadership of Roland Walls.

The aim then was for us to get a taste of life in the raw, before proceeding to eventual ordination to the priesthood. I was there with them, as I had read theology, but I did not follow them into becoming a priest. Instead I became a probation officer, which is how I came to meet my wife Margaret.

It was largely because of my short statement on Baptism, below, that I decided with my wife that we should not have our daughters baptised. I felt it was either just a formality, not to be taken that seriously; or, if taken seriously, it was too big a decision to be taken by a child or on behalf of a child.

As we know, there are many who regard Baptism as just a way of giving a name to a child. Even amongst the more enlightened, who can see this also as admitting the child into the Christian community, there are many who basically see the later ceremony of Confirmation as little more than the admission of a baptised child to adult status and to the privilege of receiving the comfort and strength of Communion. But, Communion itself is too often thought of merely as a comfort!

If, however, we look to the life of Jesus and notice the ways in which He has preceded us in all things, even in Baptism, we get a much fuller idea of the way in which the Sacraments are not only steps along the way but are also structural parts of each other—and of a frightening whole. All are part of the way of the Cross, and all point to it and are fulfilled in it. The key to this is discovered, I think, when we notice that for Jesus the fact and significance of his Baptism was present *throughout* his life. It was far from being just a beginning! Immediately after his Baptism "Jesus was led up of the Spirit into the wilderness to be tempted." and in the wilderness he rejected all ways of Messiahship except that which he chose. For him, Baptism was the turning of his face towards Jerusalem. For him, it meant accepting the painful realisation that the outcome of his Baptism was to be found only on the Cross; and as his ministry proceeds we can see this growing to an all-embracing conviction: "I have a Baptism wherewith I am baptised, and how am I straightened until it be accomplished."

Later, Jesus more explicitly links end with beginning when he asks of his disciples: "Are ye able to drink the cup that I shall drink, and to be baptised with the Baptism I am baptised with?" and they answered "We are able." Then Jesus

8

pronounced to them those terrible words: "Ye shall indeed …" And he says this also to us who come to drink of that cup.

The Communion cup should be, I am sure, not just a cup of comfort to those that drink it. For Jesus it was a cup of agony. And he, no less than we, needed to be *strengthened* before he could drink it. "If it be possible let this cup pass from me" was his cry in the garden of Gethsemane, and yet we can so easily drink of it week by week without thinking of this.

Jesus shrank from drinking that cup, for which he was baptised to drink, but "behold an angel appeared … and strengthened him." So, even in Confirmation Jesus has been before us. I therefore feel that we too should almost dread to drink of this cup, which is foreshadowed in our Baptism too and fulfilled in a life that gives itself utterly—even if this ends on a Cross.

There *may* be comfort in Communion. But also there is a repeated challenge to accept the sacrifice it signifies—as our sacrifice too. No wonder, then, that we need to be 'confirmed' before we drink it! So we find in Communion, as Jesus did, a cup to which we are committed in our Baptism—and how should *we* be "straightened until it be accomplished"!

CHAPTER THREE

The essence of Christianity

My first ever publication was this letter I sent in to the journal Theology, *written in response to an earlier letter by a fellow theologian, John Oliver. He'd been troubled by what he had read of the German philosopher Feuerbach and his best known book* The Essence of Christianity.

Oliver had said in his letter that he thought it was a matter of some urgency that the Church should write a solid refutation of Feuerbach's suggestion that "Man had made God in his own image," not the other way round. My reply, below, was published in Theology (1962).[3]

---

[3] At the time of writing it was common to use the generic term 'Man,' to stand for mankind or for men and women equally.

Dear Sir,

Barth may be right when he says that Feuerbach is "the thorn in the flesh, the bad conscience, of modern theology." But I believe we may be wasting our time if we are looking for "a convincing refutation of *The Essence of Christianity*," to quote Mr Oliver's letter in your February number.

It may be that we can find flaws in Feuerbach's exposition. But let us face the truth, we can no more prove that God is *not* Man's illusion than we can prove that God really exists.

To refute the arguments of Feuerbach no more lays the ghost of his central thesis than do the arguments of philosophers, who refute the Thomist 'proofs' [for the existence of God], disprove thereby the existence of God.

Perhaps the greatest service Feuerbach has done for Christianity has been to strip Faith of its dependence upon argument, and to leave it naked before the frightening fact that Faith itself may be Man's own need to believe, and his God his own need for a purpose bigger than life. Faith can no longer imagine that it is based upon any rational certainty, but is thrown into relief as an act of courage that commits itself utterly to God, believing him to be the maker of Man, in spite of the awful possibility that Feuerbach might be right.

Herein is the risk of Faith that makes it the act of courage it must be. We do not need to refute Feuerbach, but to incorporate his thesis as a dynamic element of a Christian *theology of Doubt*. Those who believe should now believe with their eyes open to the risk they are taking, rather than seek for protection from Doubt in some refutation of Feuerbach which, thank God, we will never find.

CHAPTER FOUR

A false security?[4]

This 'came' to me in 1962, while I was in Coventry as a student probation officer. It seemed to come from nowhere so I wrote it down, but with no thought of publication until Robinson's book hit the news (see Introduction).

Why does a Christian believe in God? Like all 'men' he is basically afraid of being alone. He is afraid of his life being without purpose, and he is afraid of being lost in his own insignificance. Life seems to him threatening and insecure, blatantly untidy with injustice. So, if this life that we endure is all of life, and if we know of no other realm where meaning can be found, then it is indeed 'a tale told by an idiot,' to escape the horror of which Man[5] must seek out some goal to look to. Man will lean on something, whether it be a life beyond death

---

[4] Casement (1962).
[5] I am continuing to use the collective 'Man' to represent mankind generally.

he can hope for, or some materialist Utopia he can work for. Or he must accept that there is no meaning and seek escape in momentary diversion, or total escape in suicide. The only remaining defence is a numbness that pretends not to care. But, if Man allows himself to think, then Voltaire was (still) right, that "If there were not a God we would need to invent one."

There is certainly need enough to find something to offer purpose in life, to give some meaning to its totality. Many who fail to find this seek then to be diverted; and, in family, in employment or recreation, they have enough to satisfy the moment. Those who are fortunate surround themselves with friends; they earn and spend and create a home, and no longer feel so alone. Others who have not even this, or find it insufficient, look for forgetfulness in drink or narcotics, in excitement or in sex, or else they just vegetate in front of an entertainment screen and wait for time to pass. Temporarily they are less aware of problems clamouring for attention, and those eternal questions that demand some answer.

Many seek this distraction. If we discover diversion alone to be not enough we will search for something more to give us reason to go on, whether it be a God that is above the troubles of this life or some substitute god within it. Even the atheist needs to find some purpose; but he merely limits the area of his search and, in claiming there to be nothing beyond this life, he thinks his quest to be satisfied by being a materialist or humanist. He can then live and die for his convictions, unaware perhaps that they are for him his credo, and their goal his god. Truly, the atheist is less without a god than many who lack his enthusiasm, for this itself is the worship he offers.

The committed Christian shares this enthusiasm and he, too, claims to have found meaning. Is this any more real than the atheist's dream, or does this again only satisfy his need? Many Christians allow no doubt about this, but they preach with overemphasis—as if to convince themselves and to silence the challenge of dissension. Some still try to defend the authority of the Bible from the advance of science, as if God would not also be Lord of science! Is it a fear that we may be mistaken in our belief, that we attempt to protect it from any attacks of doubt?

Few would deny that "Man's heart is restless."[6] But we must ask ourselves whether this is because he is made in the image of God, in whom some claim to have found their rest, or is it because he frets in a world that has no meaning? And is this search for meaning because there *is* some greater reality, which offers to satisfy it, or because life would be unbearable without some narcotic to dull the pain? So, in the interpretation of religious experience, or of any claim to believe, we are faced by the frightening choice between these two possibilities.

We can never prove or support our decision; but I believe that, in accepting this dilemma as germane to faith itself, we can discover the truth of faith—that any certainty it claims is a false security.

This dilemma soon becomes apparent if we look at some of the Christian statements about God. We regard him as Creator, but is this perhaps because of the horror of a world governed only by chance? We call him righteous, but could this be because we are appalled by the injustice of the world? We look to the miracles of Jesus as 'evidence' that he was the Christ, but may this be because we wish to be persuaded? Do we deify coincidence, to see in this the guidance of the Spirit, rather than let life seem abandoned without plan or purpose? Do we say God is love because we so greatly need to be loved?

In all of this we need our hopes to have some foundation, we need our sacrifice to be accepted, and we long to be safe and secure in believing. It may be a haven many are looking for, but they must be prepared for a precipice. For it is in our very need for a God who cares, for one who judges and redeems, and even for a heaven and a hell, that all these are

---

[6] St Augustine.

suspect. So we must face the awful possibility that the God we worship may not be God at all; and even if there be a God, we may have so coloured our image of Him, by our needs and desires, as to have almost brought Him down to our own level. We must therefore search our hearts, be ready to be stripped of any comfort in believing, and be prepared to look beyond our idea of God lest it be no more than our own projection.

Faith must know that it can never know, and must be aware of the guile of its own need to believe. And yet, like the lover for the loved one, it can still risk all and not turn back. Doubt will not relent; but it is the experience of this, as the very root of faith, that keeps faith alive and makes it the act of courage it must be.

CHAPTER FIVE

In whose image?[7]

In about 1997 I was asked if I would contribute to a book that was intended to be a follow-on from the much earlier book Objections to Christian Belief, *edited by Alec Vidler, published in 1963.*

The editor of this new book, Samuel Stein, was proposing a working title of The God of Today. *I said I really didn't like that title so he asked if I could come up with something better. I suggested* Beyond Belief, *which became the adopted title. My chapter for that book is included below. By the time I wrote it I had become a psychoanalyst.*

In writing this essay I am returning to some issues that have preoccupied me over many years. Inevitably, what I have to say will be a personal statement. I shall not be making any claim to represent the views of psychoanalysis in general, or of

---

[7] Casement (1999).

my psychoanalytic colleagues, although I hope that some may be able to agree with what I have to say.

In a spectrum of belief, I see myself neither as a believer nor as an atheist but as a 'questioning agnostic.' I arrived at this position through studying anthropology before graduating in theology. The discipline of anthropology, having opened my mind to new ways of thinking about the unknown in others, had led me to question what some might be prepared to accept on authority. In particular, I found I was no longer content with any understanding of the human condition that relied on dogma, whether that was to be found in the realm of religion or (later) in psychoanalysis. I had come to feel that everything had to be questioned, and tested against experience.[8]

My move towards this position was expressed in one of my first publications, "A False Security?" (1964), which I have included above. That paper was written at a time when I was undergoing what, in those days, was regarded as a 'crisis of faith.' I later came to realise that I had, in particular, been rebelling against the constraints of so-called certainty, towards the much greater freedom of non-certainty.

It was already dawning on me, as others (such as Feuerbach) had said before, that it is by no means certain whether we are made in the image of God, as Christians proclaim, or whether it is out of our need to believe that we may have created God in our own image. In my opinion, this dilemma cannot be resolved either by adhering to some position of religious certainty or by adopting that other kind of certainty which some atheists proclaim.

One of the responsibilities of being a psychoanalyst is to offer patients a safe and neutral space within which they can bring, and explore, whatever is their concern of the moment.

---

[8]Some of what I have to say here is to be found in my chapter "Beyond Dogma," in *Further Learning from the Patient* (1990), but here I wish to elaborate those thoughts in a slightly different direction.

This may at times include some discussion of a patient's religious belief. More often, however, patients are asking for help with regard to problems within themselves, or in their relationships to others; and, in that request for help, they do not usually represent their religion as problematic. I therefore do not consider it compatible with my role as a psychoanalyst, as I see it, to be trying to take apart what a patient believes. Instead I regard it as important that I can relate to each patient in terms of his/her own idiom. If that includes the patient's Catholicism, Judaism, Buddhism or whatever, then I think it is important to learn of that, as best I can, from the patient concerned. I therefore aim to work *with* a patient's religion rather than thinking that I have any right to challenge it.

However, what I would want to question are the extremes in religion whereby a neurotic relationship to life may be mirrored in religiosity or some religious fanaticism, which can become life-limiting rather than life-enhancing. Even then, I would aim to approach the problem with respectful caution. That religious 'posture' may, for instance, be the main thing that holds a person together. I would therefore want to begin the analytic task, with such a patient, by focusing on any day-to-day manifestations of the defensive dynamics which might also be reflected in the more extreme religious position. However, I would still not want to deprive a patient of his/her religious belief.

It does sometimes happen that the nature of a patient's belief matures as a result of work done in the analysis. For instance, it may become freed from the more primitive forms of religion, such as superstition, and from the various projections by which Man tends to reduce his conception of God to his own image.

It is all too easy for psychoanalysts, like others, to think that they know best. It therefore disquiets me when I hear of some psychoanalysts being dogmatic about religious beliefs, as if these inevitably indicate some unresolved neurotic tendency in a patient which requires further analytic endeavour to eliminate it. This is where I find my position as a questioning agnostic can be an advantage in my analytic practice. It helps me to preserve a neutrality with patients, whatever their religious position might be, as I do not claim to 'know' either that there is a God or that there is not a God. Also, I do not think that there is one truth that is higher than all others. Rather I have come to regard 'truth,' in relation to matters of the human condition, to be overdetermined, with seemingly contradictory (complementary) meanings, each having a part to play in the whole complex tapestry of life.

It has long since struck me that people who claim to stand for 'truth' frequently find themselves caught up in the primitive dynamics of splitting, denial and projection. Whether we look at religion, politics or psychoanalysis, we can find these dynamics operating: with schisms and sects inevitably forming as a consequence, each claiming to possess more of 'the truth' than others. And it is interesting that psychoanalysts, who make a study of these primitive mechanisms of defence, can also find themselves caught up in this process. People often try to enhance their own sense of certainty, as to the correctness of their own position, through viewing others as being in error.

From another point of view, as an historian of ideas, Isaiah Berlin also questions dogmatic certainty. With wry sarcasm he writes:

> Happy are those who live under a discipline which they accept without question, who freely obey the orders of leaders, spiritual or temporal, whose word is finally accepted as unbreakable law; or those who have, by their own methods, arrived at clear and unshakeable convictions about what to do and what to be that brook no possible doubt. I can only say that those who rest on such comfortable beds of dogma are victims of forms of

self-induced myopia, blinkers that may make for contentment, but not for understanding of what it is to be human. (1991, pp. 13–14)

I wrote of this in another early publication, "The Paradox of Unity," then referring to theological schisms.[9] But the same can apply to any belief systems, including those of psychoanalysis:

Much of our present theological disunity may be attributable to a natural insistence upon the unity of truth. But truth, seen from the limited perspective of finite Man, may not always be reducible to a single dimension. To see the wholeness of truth we may need to see the obverse side to that aspect which we can see, and contain the two aspects in paradoxical tension. (p. 8)[10]

And subsequently:

In the excitement of vision, in which one sees some new aspect of truth, it is all too easy to reject the old part-truth of which this new vision is but the obverse. We tend to reject the old as totally false and acclaim the new as totally true. But truth does not lie in any single part, but in that bigger whole which, within the limitations of human perspective, may only be expressible in terms of an irreconcilable paradox. (p. 8)

---

[9] "The paradox of unity," from which I am quoting, was written in the context of an ongoing ecumenical debate concerned with the manifest disunity between different Christian denominations.

[10] I am not thinking here of logical truth, in which contradiction may point to some higher 'synthesis' that could link 'thesis' and 'antithesis' to the point of resolving contradiction. Here, as indicated in the previous footnote, I am concerned more with personal truth that does not necessarily accede to the rules of logic.

I think that something like this happened in Freud's thinking about religion. His new understanding could be applied to so much, including the more primitive forms of religion, that it seemed to become common for psychoanalysts to regard religious belief as a symptom of some neurosis. Some of it no doubt is. But I think there is something amiss if all religious belief be regarded as suspect.

What a loss it would be if a patient's spirituality were to be automatically regarded as suspect by the analyst, or if a patient had to keep this away from an analysis lest it be interfered with. It is therefore to be regretted if some analysts still lack a proper respect for what may be the highest in mankind, a sense of spirituality, by which people can have a vision of the human condition that goes beyond the limits of an analyst's consulting room. However, most psychoanalysts are coming to acknowledge that they may not have all the answers, and that there is more to life than is contained within their particular view of it.

Being more familiar with the Christian narrative than with that of other religions, I have frequently been impressed by a resonance that is found in the human spirit with regard to what I have come to think of as a 'Resurrection Principle.' What I mean by this is a sequence which can be found in many areas of life, whereby new life grows out of death. There are quite different ways to explain this. At an animistic level we can see a 'resurrection' sequence in the seasons of nature. Out of the dying of autumn, and the seeming lifelessness of winter, we are greeted by the new life of spring. There is no doubt that this touches something deep in the human spirit and it is celebrated right across the spectrum of human experience: from the gardener or farmer to the poet, from painter to mystic. Of course we find it most particularly celebrated in the Christian festivals of Good Friday and Easter.

I do not know whether this Resurrection Principle is an echo of the Christian message (as some would wish to believe) or whether the Christian narrative can feel so fundamental because it parallels the triumph of new life that is found in nature, and in Man's capacity to survive profound tragedy and loss. Some certainly do, eventually, rise above the collapse of all that had formerly made life meaningful. In the course of that process there are some who feel they find new life; deepened, even enriched, by the experience of that 'death' in life. Thus, it might seem that the Resurrection Principle (as I am calling it) can be found in the consulting room just as it may be found within a religious setting.

A further dimension to this comparison between religious and analytic experience was first drawn to my attention, many years ago, by Harry Williams in *God's Wisdom in Christ's Cross* (1960). He pointed out that Jesus' view of God as Father served him only up to and including his prayer in the garden of Gethsemane: "Father, if it be possible, let this cup pass from me ..."

On the Cross, that view of God as Father was no longer adequate. What father could send his own son to be crucified? During the agony of the Cross, therefore, we hear Jesus crying: "My God, my God, why hast thou forsaken me?" Only later does Jesus come back to his more familiar use of 'Father' with his final words: "Father, into thy hands I commend my spirit."

Once again, I do not know whether life reflects a sequence pointed to by the Christian 'gospel' or whether that narrative has been so influential because others find this in their own experience also.

In the analyst's consulting room we find patients who go through a breakdown *en route* to a breakthrough: a view of life that has previously sustained them, and their own view of themselves, having since been found to be inadequate—no longer serving that purpose. For a while, sometimes for a very long while, a patient may go through the deepest despair of having lost all that had seemed to make life worthwhile.

Gradually, however, it may become possible to look beyond that deficient vision of life to something greater. In this sense, but in this quite secular setting of an analysis, patients may go through a similar experience to that described by Harry Williams: that of going through disillusionment towards something unforeseen, which may eventually be found beyond it.[11]

But, in an analysis, I know that I cannot point any patient to what could make life meaningful for them. If a renewed sense of 'life being meaningful' is ever to be adequate to a particular patient, I believe it has to be found *by* that patient; and sometimes it is found, most tellingly.

In one sense, I find my clinical experience here to be in contrast to what I find within the Christian Church. I have heard Christians preaching 'the hope of resurrection' even in the face of unspeakable tragedy. It has often seemed to me that this results, for whoever preaches this, in creating an emotional distance from the sheer pain of what another person is going through. Whilst the message surely helps to protect the preacher, it may do little for the person for whom it is intended.

A most salutary exception to this was heard during the tragedy of Dunblane[12] in 1996, when so many families were shattered by the senseless shooting of their children, while parents had been thinking that their children were safe in the care of teachers whom they trusted. It was totally appropriate that a priest said, at one of the first church services which followed: "Let there be no explanations today." Then was certainly not a time for anyone to take refuge from the shocking impact of that tragedy, least of all in theories trying to explain why

---

[11] There are echoes here of similar thoughts that have been expressed over the ages, for instance: "Who going through the vale of misery use it for a well ... they will go from strength to strength" (Psalm 84, 6); also, "the dark night of the soul" as portrayed by St John of the Cross. In addition, my attention has been drawn to a line somewhere in Sartre, where he says: "Life begins on the far side of despair."

[12] The Dunblane school massacre took place at Dunblane Primary School near Stirling, Stirlingshire, Scotland, on 13 March 1996, when Thomas Hamilton shot sixteen children and one teacher dead before killing himself. It remains the deadliest mass shooting in British history.

it happened.[13] Unfortunately, that is not what is most commonly preached within the Christian Church. More frequently I have heard the promise of eternal life proclaimed, and the triumph of Easter, in the face of each and every death.

Some may be comforted by this. But I recently heard a friend say how unhelpful it had been for her when the priest at her father's funeral had been preaching this Easter message, and how far removed it had been from what she was going through at the time.

Where then does this place the preacher in relation to tragedy and trauma? As an analyst, it worries me that a preacher (or a priest) can so readily take a distance from the pain of death and loss, or of breakdown, by immediately looking beyond it to what is thought of as some resurrection promise.

Those currently in breakdown, or the bereaved (for instance the families so afflicted in Dunblane), cannot take a distance from their pain. For some it will be with them for all their lives. And it has been said that no parent ever really recovers from the death of a child. So what happens to that continuing pain for the Christian preaching of Easter? I do not consider that it is all transformed by the promise of resurrection.

I have come to think that the reflections of Good Friday (as preached) are often followed too swiftly by the Easter message. It is almost as if Christians are invited to dwell only briefly upon the death experience of the Crucifixion, then to have their attention (almost immediately) deflected from that to the promise of Easter. Or so it can seem within the sequence of Church observance.

In real life, however, the Good Friday experience (of loss, breakdown, trauma or tragedy) is seldom, if ever, so readily resolved. When this is encountered in the consulting room, a patient's 'Good Friday' may go on for years. The analyst's task,

---

[13] For the bereaved there can be no simple relief or resolution to their grief, and most certainly not through 'explanations' of any kind.

in my opinion, is to see this through with the patient, however long that might take. There is then no place for denial or for quick reassurance.

It has come to my notice that, when I have been able to help patients to face their own worst experiences, and to survive them therapeutically, they have sometimes told me afterwards that what had helped them most had been my willingness to be alongside them during the experience. I know that I could not really have been 'with' them in this way if I had been comforting myself with the idea that they would surely come through it, as with the notion of a light at the end of the tunnel or with some other resurrection promise. For, at the time, it *feels* and *is* endless for the patient.

However much I may need to believe in the possibility of some way forward being found, beyond a patient's own worst experience, I know that I have to stay in touch with what the patient is going through, as it is at the time. That is central to the analytic endeavour, to be sufficiently in touch with the patient's experience without seeking refuge in premature 'resolution.'

In Christian devotion (unlike at the time of the Crucifixion) Good Friday now leads inevitably to the Christian Easter. Every terrible experience can thus be reduced, even limited in its significance, by the assurance of that Easter message.

There seems to be a strange contradiction. The priest, whose pastoral task includes being there for the bereaved, as for those in trouble of whatever kind, may himself be protected by his own belief in the Resurrection. This could prevent him from ever being fully alongside those he seeks to help. He may be able to give significant counsel; but, in the last analysis, I do wonder about the gap that remains between the priest and the actual experience of those to whom he seeks to administer comfort. In the Christian narrative, we are told that the function of the Incarnation, and of the Crucifixion, was to bridge precisely that gap: God became Man that he might enter most fully into Man's sufferings, alongside him in death as in life.

I think that we sometimes find a similar distancing in analyses. If an analyst places too much emphasis upon what is said, as in the interpretations given, then something important may be missed there too.

I do not question that much of the work of psychoanalysis is that of interpretation, towards patients becoming more familiar with their unconscious minds, that they may become more able to own what is theirs and to be less prone to such primitive defences as those of splitting, denial and projection. But I do not regard the analytic work of interpretation, on its own, to be enough when trying to help a patient to live through the consequences of trauma, or a patient trying to rebuild a life after breakdown.

Words alone are not always enough. I have therefore come to think that, even though analysis has been called 'the talking cure,' it is not always the analyst's interpreting that is the crux of the process. Often, what seems to have been most significant to a patient is the experience of being consistently cared for by someone who makes it his or her business to get to know that individual as deeply as may be; someone who is also prepared to be battered by the impact of the patient's distress and despair, whilst surviving this 'without collapse or retaliation' (Winnicott, 1971, p. 91). Something important, and healing, can be found in the experience of the analytic relationship itself, between the lines of what is actually said by the analyst, as well as in the words.

What helps to sustain me, when working with a patient going through a breakdown, or someone who is trying to come to terms with the experience of trauma, is the repeated discovery that some patients do eventually come through this in a way that turns out to have been creative, leading even to new life and a new vision that may lie beyond anything I could have set out to convey to them.

I know I cannot point a patient to that possible outcome, nor can I be certain if any particular patient will ever come to it. I have no guarantee so I give none.

I can, of course, call upon analytic understanding; some sense of the past that a patient may be re-experiencing in the present, or some other understanding of what is happening, to help orientate me during the analytic journey. Sometimes that understanding may also help to reorientate a patient, but there always remains a gulf between any understanding I may think that I have and the patient's own experience. (I do not believe that anyone can ever entirely bridge this gap between themselves and another.) But patients may be able to use something from what I have said, or something from my presence with them, out of which they can begin to find a bridge towards beginning to feel not so alone with what they are going through.

There is something about the analytic process that goes beyond the skill of the analyst.

I do not think it is an adequate explanation of what can happen in an analysis to imagine that it is simply a result of the work of the analyst, bringing to consciousness the troublesome aspects of the patient's unconscious mind. For if it were that alone then it would be as if the analyst were claiming to be the instrument of cure, the author of a patient's recovery.

There are some parallels here to the work of surgeons. They do not cure the patient. They may cut out what threatens a patient's life, and they carefully sew up each patient after surgery to ensure an optimum state for recovery. But the healing process lies within the patient. The analyst similarly aims to bring to consciousness what is threatening the patients' peace of mind, for them to become able to apply conscious thought to those processes that had previously been disturbing them, beyond their ken. But no patient's recovery is ever within the analyst's 'gift.'

I think that there are also parallels between what happens in an analysis and the relationship that evolves between a mother and her baby.

When all goes well, a baby's growing security is not merely a result of the mother's skill as mother: it is not solely her achievement. There is a process that occurs, between the two of them, whereby the baby may find what is needed. This is not only because the mother provides it. It is through the mother developing a sensitivity to her baby's communications so that she becomes able to recognize what is needed, and when. Only then can her provision become meaningful. That good experience, therefore, grows out of the baby discovering that communication is meaningful and that there is someone 'there' who can respond meaningfully to it.

When a mother cannot read her baby's communications, or when a baby feels that he or she is in a world without meaningful response, the relationship will become increasingly problematic until help from elsewhere becomes available or until the mother becomes better attuned to her baby. For good or for ill each enhances the contribution of the other. There is a process between them that involves them both.

The point I am trying to make here is that the outcome of a mother's attention to her baby, or of an analyst's attention to a patient, is not solely the achievement of the mother or of the analyst. It is a product of the two people interacting. But the mystery of it, in my opinion, may lie beyond each of them. We cannot be sure that we know what it is, in either setting, that contributes most to growth or to recovery.

Some people are particularly struck by the power of the analytic process that can develop between a patient and the analyst, and the sense of unconscious wisdom that can sometimes seem to inform this. It appears to 'guide' the two people engaged in that process along a journey which could not have been devised by either the analyst or the patient alone. With hindsight, it can look as if it 'had' to be that way.

Winnicott pointed out the process by which the analyst finds himself subtly drawn into failing his patient in ways that uncannily re-enact a significant 'environmental failure' in a patient's life. As a result, the patient often brings those feelings that belonged specifically to early trauma into his/her relationship to the analyst, with a fresh opportunity to work through that trauma within the analysis. "So in the end we succeed by failing, failing the patient's way" (Winnicott, 1965, p. 258). How does this come about? I do not know the answer, but I can understand why there are those who might be tempted to see the hand of some other force at work in this; that recovery from trauma can come about through ways that can seem so contrary to common sense, and which the analyst could never anticipate or plan.[14]

I am clear that my clinical work is not conducted within any religious framework. The questions I started with remain. Do we find life growing out of death as a reflection of some divine purpose, an echo of the Good Friday/Easter Day sequence? Or has the Christian narrative acquired such universal appeal because it dramatically portrays a sequence that already exists in life? For there is no doubt that we do sometimes encounter a process of recovery (from breakdown, from trauma, from loss) through which some people may even be transformed.

I still do not know whether we are made in the image of God or whether we have made God in our own image; or are these two views each a part of some greater truth? I am content to be asking these questions without needing any answer.

Not having those answers enables me to listen to my patients from a position that is (I hope) free of doctrine or dogma that could intrude upon my analytic listening. With a religious patient (of a Christian persuasion) I feel at ease in

---

[14] A very clear example of what I am saying here can be found in the description of my work with a patient (Mrs B) who, in her first year as a child, had nearly died of burns (Casement, 1985, *On Learning from the Patient*, chapter 7).

being familiar with their world view without being committed to it myself. With the non-religious, or with those of a different religious background from my own, I am at ease in learning (from them) of their quite different world view from any that has been mine.

Nevertheless, whether in the realm of religion or in that other 'religion' of psychoanalysis, I believe that we still need to watch for the ways in which we may devise dogma to suit our own personalities. In either sphere, our theory or our God should be as little made in our own image as can be. And if there be a God, then let that God be truly 'other' and beyond our own creation—as only a true God will be. Only then might we be led to a vision that lies beyond our own limitations, as our creativity is also beyond our understanding.

CHAPTER SIX

The unknown beyond the known

*I found this brief statement amongst my papers.[15] I don't recall
why I wrote it. Perhaps I was, as so often, just trying to work
out some ideas that were buzzing in my head at the time.*

I am reminded of what Christopher Bollas wrote in his first
book *The Shadow of the Object* (1987).

> There is in each of us a fundamental split between *what
> we think we know and what we know but may never be able to
> think*. In the course of the transference and countertransfer-
> ence the psychoanalyst may be able to facilitate the trans-
> fer of the unthought known into thought, and the patient
> will come to put into thought something about his being
> which he has not been able to think up until then. (p. 282)

---

[15] Some of this was first published in *Learning from Our Mistakes*
(Casement, 2002).

33

In that passage, he is writing mainly of the unknown in the patient. In this paper I am more concerned with *that which remains unknown to the analyst,* and what can happen when analysts overlook what lies beyond their own experience or understanding.

Analysts are trained not to put onto patients what does not belong to them. In particular they are trained not to attribute to patients what may belong to themselves, and trained not to use patients as 'transferential objects.' But it is not from the analyst's personal experience, or feelings, that some patients can be at risk so much as from *what may be transferred or projected onto them from other clinical experience—or from theory.* I think of this mistaken use of theory, or of one's own experience, as another kind of transference (from the analyst): some understanding from elsewhere being put onto a patient that does not necessarily apply. The problem here is that practice-wisdom naturally accrues from clinical experience, and yet this can result in sometimes not recognising when this understanding from elsewhere could be misapplied.

Though careful not to fall into the more typical forms of transference or projection, analysts can nevertheless develop a false sense of confidence in their theoretical framework and in the broad applicability of their clinical experience. Of course, in any analysis there is an essential place for theory and for clinical experience, but for some analysts (and I count myself among them) that remains secondary to the task of trying to get to understand the individual. I therefore hope not to allow myself to be pushed into seeing a patient in any particular way just because theory (or someone else) suggests that I should. Each patient is essentially unique. The individual will therefore still remain something of a mystery, however well we may eventually come to know him/her. Therefore, even though theory has a vital place in serving the work of analysis I continue to hope we will not too often be governed by it.

The value of not-knowing

Winnicott, in particular, kept reminding us of the importance of sustaining a level of not-knowing in relation to patients we are still trying to get to know, which means every patient throughout every analysis. In his own way, so did Bion.

> Instead of trying to bring a brilliant, intelligent, knowledgeable light to bear on obscure problems, I suggest we bring to bear a diminution of the 'light'—a penetrating beam of darkness; a reciprocal of the searchlight ... The darkness would be so absolute that it would achieve a luminous, absolute vacuum. So that, if any object existed, however faint, it would show up very clearly. Thus, a very faint light would become visible in maximum conditions of darkness. (1990: 22–23)

Some patients come into analysis with shattering experiences locked in their minds, or with inconceivable chaos and confusion spilling into consciousness. If analysts are truly to engage with these experiences, rather than defending themselves with familiar theory, they need to look for that faint light of meaning in the midst of all that may seem like non-sense. Some things presented by the patient may threaten to be upsetting also for the analyst, disturbing the analyst's view of himself/herself or preconceptions about theory or technique.

For instance, it may be the primitive registration of early trauma that requires fresh understanding, even though it could defy established theories of memory. Maybe we have to take more seriously a notion of body-memory to make sense of this. Or, we may be faced by details of trauma that we would much prefer to regard as unbelievable, such as the extremes of sexual abuse that have been described as 'satanic.' It is much more comfortable for the analyst to cling to theories of unconscious phantasy,[16] or to diagnose psychosis in the patient, than to dare to believe that *occasionally* there may be some truth in these terrible accounts of abuse.[17] And, at the opposite extreme, it may be ineffable experience (religious and/or spiritual) that should prompt us to wonder whether psychoanalytic theory can really explain *all* of this away. In situations such as these, we may encounter areas of experience that go beyond anything we have any direct knowledge of, or adequate theory to encompass.

Equally, we may find ourselves used by a patient in ways that go beyond what we regard as proper to an analysis, or in ways that profoundly test our usual technique. For instance, I was persuaded by one patient (for quite long periods) not to interpret at all. Instead, I listened (mostly in silence) for session after session, hardly being allowed to speak, and then being allowed only to register that I had recognised some essence of what I was being told. It felt very strange and as if I was being rendered entirely impotent. Some might say that I had colluded with the controlling demands of my patient. But the analysis continued and later began to prove to have been more fruitful than when I had still imagined that I should be the one to provide understanding. And it is not insignificant that this patient's mother was profoundly deaf.

---

[16] I continue to use this spelling to distinguish between unconscious phantasy, as in Isaacs (1948), and fantasy which can be a conscious imagining.
[17] See also "On the Wish Not to Know" (Casement, 1994).

CHAPTER SEVEN

Certainty and non-certainty[18]

In 1962 I was asked to preach a sermon in the town of Oldham, in the north of England, where I had been doing a placement as a student social worker. My sermon was to be one of a series of four, on the traditional themes for Advent, *The Four Last Things*: death, judgement, hell and heaven. I was asked to preach on hell.

I no longer have the sermon I gave on that day but I remember that I was giving a view of hell as self-made. I suggested that we are offered God's love, an unconditional love, to which we may respond or not. We are left free to make whichever response we choose. Often we may turn our backs, feeling unable to respond to it or refusing to accept the love that is offered. We may refuse this love out of arrogance, believing that we can do without it. Or we may claim to know better than God, in seeing ourselves as being beyond the reach of that love

---

[18] From chapter 11 in *Learning from Life* (Casement, 2006).

through being unworthy of it. How could we receive the grace of God? Should we not first become deserving of it through our own good works? Yet another kind of arrogance.

The hell we may experience does not have to be a hell that we are condemned to by a vengeful God. The vengeful God we hear about may simply be an invention of our own imagination, being often so much nearer to how we are, in ourselves, than the all-loving God that we are invited to turn to. Therefore, when we feel we are 'in hell' this may be a hell of our own making, beyond which there may yet be a loving and grieving God who waits for the return of those who turn their backs upon his love.

The seeds of that view of hell were sown during my time at Cambridge. For instance, while I was still there, I heard Mervyn Stockwood preach on Dostoyevsky's 'The Grand Inquisitor.' I don't remember the sermon but I have never forgotten being introduced to that visionary chapter in *The Brothers Karamazov* (1879–80). It has remained an inspiration for me ever since. Dostoyevsky highlights there some of the things that have gone wrong with institutionalised Christianity. He also shows a prophetic insight into some of the dynamics in communist Russia.

Dostoyevsky describes an imaginary sequence that takes place in Spain, in Seville, during the Inquisition. It is set "at the moment when, a day before, nearly a hundred heretics had been burnt all at once by the cardinal, the Grand Inquisitor, *ad majoram gloriam Dei*" (p. 291).[19] Into this scene the risen 'Christus' (the living Christ) appears. "He appeared quietly, inconspicuously, but everyone—and that is why it is so strange—recognized him" (p. 291). People are gathered in great numbers around the cathedral to do homage to the Grand Inquisitor, for having (yet again) saved the Church from heresy. But then they see the Christus amongst them.

---

[19] All the page numbers in this chapter refer to the Penguin Classics edition of *The Brothers Karamazov*, translated by David Magarshack (1958).

> The people are drawn to him by an irresistible force,
> they surround him, they throng him, they follow him.
> He walks among them in silence. ... He stretches forth his
> hands to them, blesses them, and a healing virtue comes
> from contact with him, even with his garments. (p. 291)

Further scenes repeat moments from the life of Jesus, as recorded in the Gospels. A blind man receives his sight again. They bring him a child who is being carried in an open coffin. He speaks to the child, once again saying those words "*Talitha cumi*," and she's raised from the dead. At this moment the Grand Inquisitor passes by and sees what is happening. He recognises the Christus and orders that he be arrested.

For the rest of this extraordinary chapter the Grand Inquisitor is with this figure, in the prison where he has been sent, questioning and challenging him. The prisoner remains silent. What the Grand Inquisitor is saying throughout this monologue is that Jesus had got things wrong:

> Everything ... has been handed over by you to the Pope
> and, therefore, everything is now in the Pope's hands,
> and there's no need for you to come at all now—at any
> rate do not interfere. (p. 294)

The Grand Inquisitor explains that, though Jesus had offered to make people free, they do not want to be free. They cannot bear being unsure. They want certainty in belief, and instructions for life that are beyond question.

> For fifteen centuries we've been troubled by this free-
> dom, but now it's over and done with for good. ... I want
> you to know that now—yes, today—these men are more
> than ever convinced that they are absolutely free, and yet
> they themselves have brought their freedom to us and
> humbly laid it at our feet. But it was we who did it. (p. 294)

The Grand Inquisitor goes on. Jesus had refused the only ways that could have worked with the masses, when he had rejected the temptations presented to him in the wilderness. He could have turned stones into bread. People who are free do not share their bread. Instead, the Grand Inquisitor says that the Church now takes people's freedom *and* their bread. It is now the Church that distributes the bread. He continues:

> Man, so long as he remains free, has no more constant and agonizing anxiety than to find as quickly as possible someone to worship. But Man seeks to worship only what is incontestable; so incontestable, indeed, that all men at once agree to worship it all together. (pp. 297–298)

> It is this need for *universal* worship that is the chief torment of every man individually and of mankind as a whole from the beginning of time. For the sake of that universal worship they have put each other to the sword. They have set up gods and called upon each other, "Give up your gods and come and worship ours, or else death to you and to your gods!" (p. 298)

> Only he can gain possession of men's freedom who is able to set their conscience at ease. With the bread you were given an incontestable banner: give them bread and man will worship you, for there is nothing more incontestable than bread; but if at the same time someone besides yourself should gain possession of his conscience—oh, then he will even throw away your bread and follow him who has ensnared his conscience. (p. 298)

> You wanted man's free love so that he should follow you freely, fascinated and captivated by you. Instead of the strict ancient law, man had in future to decide for himself with a free heart what is good and what is evil, having only your image before him for guidance. But did it never occur to you that he would at last reject and call in question even your image and your truth, if he were

40

weighed down by so fearful a burden as freedom of choice? (p. 299)

There are three forces, the only three forces that are able to conquer and hold captive forever the conscience of these weak rebels for their own happiness—these forces are: miracle, mystery, and authority. You rejected all three. (p. 299)

We have corrected your great work and have based it on *miracle, mystery, and authority*. And men rejoiced that they were once more led like sheep and that the terrible gift [of freedom] which had brought them so much suffering had at last been lifted from their hearts. (p. 301)

The Grand Inquisitor reminds the Christus that, if he had accepted the temptations set him by the devil in the wilderness:

You would have accomplished all that man seeks on earth, that is to say, whom to worship, to whom to entrust his conscience and how at last to unite all in a common, harmonious, and incontestable ant-hill, for the need of universal unity is the third and last torment of men. (p. 301)

The Grand Inquisitor's monologue ends. The story continues:

He waited for some time for the Prisoner's reply. His silence distressed him. He saw that the Prisoner had been listening intently to him all the time, looking gently into his face and evidently not wishing to say anything in reply. The old man would have liked him to say something, however bitter and terrible. But he suddenly approached the old man and kissed him gently on his bloodless, aged lips. That was all his answer. (p. 308)

The old man showed him to the door: "Go, and come no more—don't come at all—never, *never*!" (p. 308)

I have quoted extensively from this chapter because I think it spells out so much that is true about organised religion and, in time, also about any totalitarian state. It is remarkable how similar the dynamics between them can be, but I think the chapter points to much else that is also true.

Throughout the history of the Christian Church we see signs of people improving on the message given them by Jesus. Men prefer to have their God made in their own image.

In the service of controlling the masses in the name of religion, it might well be more effective to have a vengeful God, with the fear of damnation and the fires of hell, to bind men to a fearful observation of the rules set out by the Church, than to risk losing control over the masses. Never mind, perhaps, that this reduces much of religious observation to a superstitious fear of the consequences of failure. The masses are more readily brought to heel by fear than by any vision of a different way of life that is *not* governed by laws, but is a matter of individual freedom.

Where superstition reigns there will more often be full churches. Just look at the few numbers of those who still respond to that invitation to freedom, so scorned by the Grand Inquisitor, for which he criticises the Christus. That freedom is more than most people can bear.

In the Grand Inquisitor chapter, nevertheless, we still get a sense of the untainted message presented to the disciples in the life and death of Jesus. He seemed to have been pointing them beyond the limitations of the ancient law, as passed on to them from the Old Testament. Jesus had been presenting people with a sense of a life that could be self-giving for others, a vision to inspire them and to show them a different way. Those that could respond to this vision would not need to be *told* how to live their lives. Instead, people were invited to find their own way to respond to it. So it would only be those who could not see it, or who could not respond to it,

42

who might need to be told how to live the 'good life,' though all might need help in dealing with the obstacles in themselves that get in the way of a fuller response to that vision.

I believe that Dostoyevsky points out the damage that has been done by the institutionalising of Christianity, with its accumulation of new laws and the listing of sins committed in breaking them, with the related system of Confession and Absolution—all under the authority of the Church.

I believe this passage also shows the effect of the divisions that have grown up from the attempts, by many, to define their own versions of how the Church should be, each saying to others: "Give up your gods and come and worship ours." Throughout the history of the Church we find this splitting over differences, each schism being man-made but each claiming to know the mind of God better than others do. Wars have been fought, and terrible atrocities committed, in the name of these rival claims.

Much, if not everything, of what is claimed to be in the name of God is what men have created. This is what Dostoyevsky is pointing to, in saying that the authorities have corrected Jesus' errors, building a system more suited to the masses so that they might at last be united 'in a common, harmonious ant-hill.'

A brief experience of fundamentalism

In *Learning from Life* (chapter 2) I wrote that for a while I allowed myself to feel that I was in safe hands when I was being persuaded to join an evangelical group that claimed me as a convert. Behind them, I was being assured, was the ultimate guide—God. I was being promised much. I was promised forgiveness. I was promised that I would always be safe in 'the everlasting arms of the Father.' How very appealing it was for an adolescent looking for certainty. I did not care that my mind was being taken over by others. I thought I was being brought to 'the truth.' I should therefore welcome giving up the error of my ways, or my wrong thinking. Also, when I doubted, I could pray to be helped in my unbelief.

In addition, I now realise, I was able to disown my own doubts by addressing doubts that I could find in others. The evangelicals saw themselves as the holders of ultimate truth: truth for all the world. We were therefore encouraged to seek out those who needed to be given 'the truth' as we had been given it. The world was seen in black and white terms. But the dynamics of certainty were still unknown to me. I did not recognise that I was being brainwashed.

The appeal of certainty

We are readily attracted to a notion of being certain. We like to believe that we are right. This can make life seem simple, as anyone who disagrees can be assumed to be in the wrong. Also, when a group forms around a shared belief, the group dynamic that develops will often reinforce a sense of rightness. Especially as regards religion, people claim to be on the side of the right and the good. Then, in the name of truth, they proselytise amongst those who think differently, and it is easy to feel specially blessed when one is on a crusade for one's own idea of 'the truth.' Like the Grand Inquisitor, people have fought wars and burned heretics for the greater glory of God. But what is missing is a proper realisation that what is right for one person is not necessarily right for all. What feels true to me does not have to be true for you.

Not long after World War II, I had a salutary lesson with regard to this idea of fighting on the side of right. I was staying briefly with an Austrian family in Salzburg, and was shown the funeral card of a son who had died as a pilot during the war. He had been shot down by the Russians. On this card were written the familiar lines: "I have fought the good fight and I have kept the faith." But, what an irony! Those same lines were used for many of our own war dead. In Ireland also, the two warring sides have felt passionately that they have each been 'fighting the good fight,' with terrible acts being done in the name of their separate ideas of truth; and we find a similar dynamic throughout the world.

Some dynamics of certainty

The appeal of certainty has roots that go very deep. We should not be surprised at this, for we are born into the uncertainty of a world so different from that in which we were conceived. In this uncertain world we have to find such security as we can. So, from the start, we have had to believe that we were being taken care of by the 'best mother in the world,' regardless of anything that might bring that belief into question.

Also, in the service of that illusion we soon learned to split off whatever experience challenged that idea of security, thus inventing a 'good' mother from whom only good could come, and a 'bad' mother to whom all bad experience could be attributed. One version of that is to be found in the concepts of a Kleinian 'good breast' and a 'bad breast'; and other versions abound in tales of the 'good fairy' and the 'wicked witch.' Adult versions of these illusions can be found in the notion of idealised parents, which may also be projected onto God the Father and the Blessed Virgin Mary, over against the devil—that ultimate 'not me' wicked one.

It was part of our earliest system of defence, to protect us from conflict, that we built up a split view of the world. This included a split between 'me' and 'not me.' Thus the outside world, insofar as we were then aware of it, could seem to be a tidy enough affair with good and bad each in its place. Similarly, our own 'inside' could be thought of as the place where good should be, and some bits of 'the outside' as the places into which all bad could be expelled. So, in the service of security we developed these splits.

With such systems of certainty in place, we might seem to be protected from some of the unavoidable conflicts of living—in particular the conflicts of ambivalence, uncertainty and indecision. For within a system of unquestioned belief, as children or as adults, we may feel that we are able to know where we are and how we stand in the world.

The defence systems of childhood frequently persist in other apparently more adult worlds. Religion naturally becomes a playground for primitive defences, in particular those of idealisation, splitting, projection and denial. People in politics also make much of these, our own party being regarded as the fount of all that is good and the other party being blamed for whatever is wrong in the world. The field of psychoanalysis is also not free from this.

Most of us who work in the psychoanalytic world would wish to believe that we have been well enough analysed not to resort to such primitive defences. It is to be hoped that, as individuals, we may become less prone to do so. But when we identify ourselves with a particular group that has developed around a given theory, we often revert to splitting and projection. We find here too a tendency to believe that the views of our own group are right and the views of others mistaken. Or we see some old theoretical position as now superseded by another, sometimes presented as the new way. Inevitably, schisms develop in psychoanalytic societies also.

In belonging to a group of like-minded colleagues, we may find some respite from the aloneness of the consulting room. Those of us who work long hours, without much contact with anyone other than our patients, may not want to question too much the basis of such harmony as we find in a like-minded group. There we can find a sense of cohesion around a common belief system.

Hardly a single psychoanalytic society has been able to remain coherent and undivided. It has been said that it is only here in Britain, maybe because of our national readiness to compromise, that the British Psychoanalytical Society has not split. We have somehow held together three groups under one roof. But within this nominally single society, fundamental differences remain unresolved.

So where do we each stand in relation to our own belief system in psychoanalysis? Do we believe that we 'know,' or that we belong to the group that has it most right? And if we do not believe that, where are we? Are we merely doubters, sceptics or muddled thinkers? How do the more sure relate to those who do not claim to be so sure? Are they respectful of that difference, or are they contemptuous of it? What then is the dynamic that exists between these different positions? With regard to this, are we analysts really so different from people in the field of politics and religion?

Religion and superstition

It is tempting for psychoanalysts to believe they have been able to analyse religion away.

There is a serious point being made by these critics of religion, and it is partly for this reason that I considered myself an agnostic for most of my time as a practising psychoanalyst. However, I did not altogether divorce myself from my roots, having once thought that I might become a priest and having graduated in theology. I therefore chose to think of myself as a 'Christian agnostic.'[20] At least I could never assume the position of an atheist who claims to *know* that there is no god.

I cannot know that there *is* or that there *is not* a god; a creator and/or an intelligent mind behind the infinity of the cosmos, and the amazing beauty and diversity that we find in nature.

---

[20] By 'Christian agnostic' I was acknowledging that I continued to be influenced by my familiarity with Christian thinking and practice, but without the same conviction in believing as those calling themselves Christians.

Can it all be put down to chance? Can it all be put down to evolution?

I recall, with some discomfort, a time when I was present at a training committee that was deliberating a candidate's readiness to qualify. All the reports were in favour. The only dissenting voice came from one person who knew the candidate continued to practise his religion and said: "He obviously needs more analysis as he is still caught up in superstition." Despite this reservation, the candidate was allowed to qualify, but it continued to trouble me that Freud's prejudice against religion was still so active. Much later I was prompted to rethink my own prejudices against religion.

Still beyond our ken

In 2000 our second daughter was getting married and I asked our local vicar if his church could be used for the wedding ceremony. He agreed, but added that he thought at least one member of the family should begin to attend some of the services at the church. I chose to be the one to attend.

A particularly important experience for me, in my wife's planning for this wedding, was the fact that she had the inspired idea of asking my old friend (and former enemy) David, who had married my 'first love,' to conduct the service. This was a most healing choice. It gave him a role in relation to all of us. He had long since lost his first wife, who had died young as had been expected. Now he was to be with us in our local church, as a priest, conducting the marriage service for our daughter's wedding. He, whom I had once hated with a passionate jealousy, was to be with us once again as a friend to me and now a friend to all my family.

In attending this church (All Hallows, Gospel Oak), in place of the seemingly unthinking recital of liturgy I'd remembered in many other churches, I was surprised to find thoughtful and thought-provoking sermons. I also found a sense of relief at being back in a religious setting I had scorned for so many years. I was glad to be once again confronted by mystery and a sense of transcendence, both of which seem to have little place in psychoanalysis.

I had then to be asking myself whether psychoanalysis can really claim to have the last word on matters of religion. That would mean standing in judgement over many great minds, and I could no longer assume them all to be mistaken. It would also go against much of my own thinking about people in my clinical work, through whom I have come to an increasing sense of the otherness of the other.

In church there can also be a sense of otherness, an awareness that the god (or God) being worshipped is not necessarily all man-made. Maybe, after all, there is something 'other' that draws people to bow before transcendence, before mystery. Maybe we need to acknowledge that there really could be more in life than we can know or understand, recognising that the ineffable will always lie beyond our ken. Maybe there is also something to celebrate in this.

I am not suggesting that I have returned to where I was when I turned my back upon the Church and all it seemed to stand for. I am beginning to find a different place for me in a larger scale of things, no longer feeling that I can be an analyst who claims to be above it all. Once again I too can bow before what we do not understand.

Our elder daughter happens to have an interest in Buddhism. This has also led me to think further about the unknowable, and the meaning of life. And I have noticed a much greater sense of reverence in a Buddhist temple than I usually find in a Western church. I don't believe we need to be divided by our different loyalties.

Looking at the history of religion, we repeatedly find that divisions are set up in the name of different creeds, the different views on what lies beyond our understanding. But people naturally prefer to find agreement with their own kind, seeking a 'universal unity' such as Dostoyevsky wrote about. So, when people agree upon definitions, of what this group or that group holds to be 'the truth,' inevitable divisions then develop and wars are still fought to put down those who dare to believe differently.

I have therefore found myself thinking that Unity does not necessarily have to be found in the unity of rational thinking, where logic holds sway and definitions determine whether others hold to our own view of the truth, or are against it. Perhaps, unknown to ourselves, we are joined in a different way, as the spokes of a wheel are joined at the centre. Maybe, without knowing it, the long-established faiths are drawn towards a centre that remains beyond our ken, even though each faith lies in a different position in relation to that unknowable centre. Maybe each has a sense of some aspect of a greater truth that we all reach for, over which no single group has monopoly.

It is, after all, the human dimension that divides each faith from the others, each claiming its own version of the truth to be the only one for the world. It is this human determination to grasp at a particular idea of the divine, and to claim ownership, that creates the definitions that divide us. Just possibly there is something that lies entirely beyond us that will always defy definition, which cannot be grasped or owned. I have therefore come to believe there is still a place for bowing before mystery.

A few years ago I was telephoned by a fellow training analyst, inviting my wife and me to a Christmas midnight mass in a well-known church. We agreed to go together. Before entering, I asked my colleague if it would be embarrassing to find me going up to the altar to receive Communion. I was surprised and delighted to discover that my colleague would also be receiving Communion. I don't know whether either of us believed all that those around us might claim to believe, but it seemed entirely appropriate that some analysts could still be looking outside the usual realm of their profession, to share a sense of something 'beyond,' before which they too could bend a knee.

Some readers might think I am revealing here that I need more analysis, like the candidate whose qualification could have been held up. Or might it be that there really is a place, even in our consulting rooms, for a sense of something that could be bigger than either of the two people who are engaged in the analytic process? We know that this process develops between the patient and the analyst, but who or what brings about this process? Is it the analyst? Is it the patient? Or is it something that develops between the two, which sometimes shows a wisdom that seems to come from elsewhere?

Non-certainty

I return to something I learned from a patient and included in an earlier book:

> It is very interesting to find that, in *Sanskrit*, the word for 'certainty' is the same as the word for 'imprisonment.' And the word for 'non-certainty' is the same as the word for 'freedom.' (Casement, 2002, p. 16)

I see *non-certainty* as very different from *uncertainty*. Non-certainty is not about indecision, nor is it about ignorance. Rather, we can make a positive choice to remain, for the time being, *non*-certain. This can help to keep us open to meaning that we have not yet arrived at. I also try to return to a position of non-certainty when I notice that I am beginning to claim too much sureness in relation to others, because anyone who is too sure can quickly become someone who is sure that those who disagree must be in the wrong.

Psychoanalysts sometimes inhibit the discovery of fresh understanding by being too sure about the understanding they claim to have. When we are too sure, we are in danger of becoming slaves to our own thinking and to our own preferred theories. We may then become trapped by preconception, which can blind us to what else may lie beyond the limits of our current thinking.

Of course patients need to find that the analyst can sometimes be sure. I believe that a particular occasion for such firmness is when the analysis, or the patient, is felt to be at risk. The patient then needs to know that the analyst has a clear sense of this.

There will also be occasions when confrontation is called for, and there too the analyst has to be able to stand firm. But, in the process of trying to understand what is not yet understood, I believe that the analytic process is often better served by our maintaining a sense of non-certainty until we are better able to understand. What is then understood may not always fit into what could be expected on the basis of established theory or other clinical experience.

With this discipline, of returning to non-certainty when necessary, psychoanalysis can continue to be the liberating process that it has the potential to be. It can be the very opposite to brainwashing. It is also entirely different from the bullying or pressurising that one person might put upon another to bring the victim of that treatment into line with the bully's own ways of thinking. I believe that it is towards this freedom, in thinking and in being, that psychoanalysis offers a way. And it is within this freedom, I believe, that the future of psychoanalysis lies.

Paradoxically, non-certainty does not have to be a defence against ignorance, or lack of experience. It takes the confidence of experience for an analyst to be able to maintain non-certainty as the creative mindset it can be. This is the challenge we are constantly having to face in this 'impossible profession.'

Conclusion

I have only been able to approach the title of this chapter indirectly, and that of the chapter before. Of course we cannot know 'the unknown' before we meet it. My point is that we may never meet it in analysis if we approach the analytic task *only* in terms of what we already know. The best we can do, therefore, is to recognise the problems that stem from knowledge, whether that is based upon our experience of life, our clinical experience, or our training. Sometimes it is beyond all of this that the unknown of a patient lies, especially when it does not fit with what we have previously known. But when that unknown is found to have the 'light' that Bion speaks of, *a light that does not come from the analyst but from the patient*, we have something important to learn from it.

Finally, as I have often said, if we really engage with something previously unknown to us *we are changed by it*. This is because we are challenged by it. We are challenged in how we view ourselves, in how we view the patient, in how we view our theory and our technique. If we resist that challenge we may miss the significance of whatever threatens our present thinking. And what might we be doing to a patient, who needs us to risk being extended in how we think and how we work, if we cannot meet him or her openly in areas of experience for which we do not yet have any adequate map?

However, if we are careful to follow the patient, and do not attempt to lead, we can afford to venture beyond the familiar. We can even risk getting out of our depth, and sometimes getting lost, until we later discover where we have been.

CHAPTER EIGHT

Ikons—ancient and modern: looking towards the unknown[21]

I am unable to clarify what prompted me to get into this rather strange piece of writing. The reflections that follow came unbidden. There was no agenda and no context beyond that of playing with some ideas that might be interesting.

Something that psychoanalysis has in common with religion is that, in each, we are confronted by the unknown. In each we attempt to know the unfamiliar through the familiar. In each we may become misguided by our own imagining and preconception. In each we find a restless wish to find answers to questions that trouble us. In each we find an unease at not knowing. But what is it that we then claim to know?

Ikons or icons? What on earth am I talking about? Well, I hope it may become clear that this is quite a good question: 'What on earth?'

---

[21] Casement (2018).

In this computer age, we are very familiar with the notion of icons. Our computers are full of them, and without them we would not be able to find our way around. Computers would remain mostly beyond our ken; even unusable. So, we turn to icons almost daily. Today's icons represent what we expect to find. We mostly know what we are looking for, and what may help us to find it, so we go to an icon hoping it will lead us into familiar territory.

I now wish to consider a paradoxical use of this notion of icon, as with the Greek word *ikon*.

We mostly prefer to have our feet firmly upon the ground, to have a sense of knowing where we are; not too much to be faced by what we do not know. But *ikons*, in another setting, may point us especially towards the unknown and to all that remains beyond our knowing, and beyond our impatient grasp to understand.

As T. S. Eliot pointed out: "Human kind cannot bear very much reality," so we try to move beyond it into mystery. Equally, we cannot bear too much mystery, so we often seek to tie down what is not yet known, believing it will eventually become known.

We seem, mostly, to have lost any appetite for standing in the presence of mystery. Instead, we can look back over some thousands of years where we can study a record of Man's attempts at grounding the unknown, in trying to make sense of a sense of God, and often we can feel superior in our criticism of such foolishness.

In many biblical texts we find frequent examples of people, in effect, *making God in their own image* even though there is a familiar creed that states the opposite: that God, we are told, "made Man in his own image." In the name of those primitive notions of 'God' we can see a never-ending series of disasters.

Repeatedly we are told that "God is on our side," that God will slay our enemies, and will condemn the sinner to purgatory, or to Hell, and much else. With such a notion of God, we can see people's views on justice, and their own wishes for retribution upon enemies, reflected in many such passages of the Bible and in the Koran also.

All of this is written in those 'holy' texts. Who are we to question that? Except we should question it, *all of it*, because history is full of divisions and wars, and many atrocities, much of them inspired by this dangerous thing we call 'religion.'

So, where does the old notion of an ikon come into this?

Alongside the terrible history of religious wars, and much else that we can condemn, there has been a long tradition, particularly in the Greek and Russian Orthodox faiths, of a veneration of *ikons*; those otherworldly images that look beyond life as we know it. What does that mean?

It could mean a worrying attachment to concrete images, a kind of substitute for the gods of Greek and Roman mythology, being venerated as if they were in themselves holy and to be treated as such. But none of that seems to lead anywhere useful, for that might be just another example of primitive thinking and superstitious observance.

But if we allow ourselves to look beyond those concrete images, just maybe we can get a sense of something quite other in the notion of an *ikon*.

We may be able to recognise those ancient *ikons* as early attempts at giving expression to the inexpressible; pointing towards a sense of transcendence that can take us beyond ourselves towards something quite other. But can we bear to remain unable to define this, unable to grasp this, and yet be prepared to remain in awe of that which remains beyond ourselves and beyond our understanding?

The would-be scientist in each of us may retreat from such thinking, being scornful of those who seem to be so naive as to consider a sense of transcendence, in our midst and beyond it. It has become a present-day trend for atheists, especially militant atheists, to stand in judgement of those who seem to be so misguided as to dare to reflect upon what atheists would no longer even consider. After all, atheists seem to 'know' in ways an agnostic cannot know: they *know* that there is no such thing as God. They can be eloquent in pointing to examples that are there to find, which help them to build their sense of certainty that there is no God.

That has become the atheist's creed, held with a certainty that many faithful believers would not claim. But there are 'believers,' private rather than militant, who feel they are unable to possess a similar certainty about their beliefs. And certainty, in any case, can only ever lead to divisions and conflict.

Those people of certainty, who are gripped by whatever position of sureness they have chosen to embrace, often stand up for what they have adopted as the banner under which they will fight. Some will even give up their lives to protect what they have chosen to stand for. Consequently, we find history is awash with the blood of religious conflict. But none of that which has been done in the name of religion has to do with the mystery of a God that lies beyond our grasp.

One exception to what I am saying could be claimed by those who believe that God, in that man Jesus, came to reveal more of what lies beyond our understanding: beyond our attempts to grasp a God that cannot be grasped. And yet, most of the attempts at describing that new sense of God have also been tarnished by that familiar tendency to create God in one's own image.

Thus, even the Christian message has been spoiled by a continuing projection onto God of what we expect to find, along with a wish to codify and to define. For instance, we find examples, even in the New Testament, of God still being regarded as condemning those who offend him, with words of retribution by God being ascribed to Jesus by the writers of those Gospels.

However it has been suggested by recent scholarship (for instance, Houlden, 1992, 2002) that those 'pre-Christian' insertions in the Gospels were most probably included to reflect a continuing (primitive) belief in a vengeful God, for it is likely that there were still many who remained reluctant or unwilling to move beyond their own primitive view of a god of their own making.

It thus continues to be difficult for many Christians to move beyond the seeming security of a world thought to be governed by the structures of their own sense of morality and justice, rather than have life remaining largely incomprehensible, as in being pointed towards a God who even loves sinners rather than condemning them.

It is to such a vision as that, and the mystery of it, that the religious *ikon* points, inviting us to contemplate the inexpressible mystery of that most ultimate Other: a sense of God that we can barely comprehend, that cannot be grasped or limited within the arrogance of our own thinking.

Through all of this we see people struggling to know what cannot be known, claiming that they can know better than others do. There will always be those who think they possess the ultimate truth, more than others. But do they? Man's arrogance in the face of mystery, and in the face of others who think differently, will never let up.

So, what does this have to do with psychoanalysis?

I think it lies at the very heart of psychoanalysis, either as it is or how it could be. For we should always be challenged by the otherness of the Other, in each and every patient.

Let us consider how we set about trying to understand the Other we are being challenged to engage with. Which *ikons*, or icons, do we look to as we continue upon our analytic journey with each patient?

The task before us can be daunting. So, of course, we look for guidance; and there is usually no lack of it available. We find, as in Freud, pressures towards understanding the unfamiliar in terms of the familiar. Many such icons will seem to lead us towards established ways of understanding what is not yet known. And it can be so seductive.

We don't usually like to feel at sea in the presence of whatever remains strange to us. So we can feel drawn towards any offered insight that may seem to lead us beyond our sense of impotence in the face of what remains unknown. Too often, it can seem to be helpful that there are those who claim to speak with the authority of their experience, giving us short cuts towards understanding, even if that leads us into *mis*-understanding.

Nevertheless, each 'icon' of theory, or of prior experience, can feel like a light that shines in the darkness. It can seem to offer us light to shine upon the unknown that we still encounter with each patient. But we need to be wary about any fresh light we seem to be able to throw upon what is not yet familiar. We can too readily become beguiled by our own wish to think we understand, when it might be more productive if we were able, instead, to develop a patience in our not yet knowing.

So where do we choose to stand when we are confronted by the otherness of each patient we meet? Will we be following the familiar trace of icons that seem to show us the way? Or can we bear to remain in a place of awe, as when contemplating an ancient *ikon*, until fresh understanding may emerge from such contemplation as this? And can we bear to find sufficient patience in our unknowing? Or might we be drawn into a present-day tendency to seek a sense of sureness in our haste to understand or to be understood?

Let us also keep in mind that the ancient *ikon* not only points outwards, beyond the known, towards what remains unknown. The central figure in any *ikon* also looks penetratingly into the eyes of the beholder, pointing to the unknown in each of us. Therein lies the creative potential of psychoanalysis when we dare to allow some meeting to occur with the not yet known of the other, maybe engaging also with the not yet known within ourselves.

CHAPTER NINE

De Profundis

Out of the depths have I cried unto thee, O Lord.
(Psalm 130, v.1)

I will not claim that I was always appealing to God when life was most dark for me, but I have often wondered about the strange fact that some of the most productive episodes in my life have emerged from the lowest of times.

In choosing to read theology, and thereby to have Harry Williams as my supervisor and tutor in Trinity College, Cambridge, I seem to have anticipated a time when Harry's influence would be most especially profound for me. I mention this in *Learning from Life* (2006).

> One of the things I had learned from Harry was his notion of *breakdown* as *breakthrough*, he having had his own quite serious breakdown for which he had received some years of psychotherapy.

Harry saw [his] breakdown as having provided him with an opportunity to break free of old ideas, old ways of being, old dogma and a search for certainty, to find beyond these a chance to discover life afresh and a new meaning in life. His view of this had fired my imagination, but I never realized how it might eventually come to be my own experience. (p. 34)

Later, in 1961–62, I found myself retained as an inpatient (my breakdown) in the Warneford Psychiatric Hospital, Oxford, and I remembered Harry's own experience of breakdown. As I say further in *Learning from Life*:

It was during this prolonged period of despair that I wrote to my former tutor, Harry Williams, knowing that he too had been through a time of breakdown. I still remember his reply. In his letter he said: "The Good Friday experience can go on for a long time and it can feel as if it will go on forever. But believe me, Patrick, in time you will come through this to your own Easter Day. And things will not be the same as before." How right he was. (p. 39)

I have continued to be struck by the relevance of what Harry had written to me. And I later came to understand more of that death-into-life sequence, or what I came to think of as illustrating a *resurrection principle* (see above p. 22). We find this too in the Gospel of St John.

Truly, truly, I say to you, except a corn of wheat fall into the ground and die, it stays alone: but if it die, it brings forth much fruit. (St John 12:24)

In so many areas of life, I now realise, we need to be able to tolerate the 'death' of what we may formerly have regarded as essential to our well-being, or seen as fundamental to our own ways of thinking or existing. We may then find that, beyond the death of what we had previously clung to, we may become newly open to much we had not until then even contemplated.

Strangely, I have come to see how much of what eventually became central to my life, and to my subsequent work, has grown out of my own breakdown and eventual recovery.

I had to let go of my intense emotional dependence, which had led to my 'first love' having to escape from me to another more healthy relationship elsewhere.

I also had to let go much of my former ways of thinking. I have therefore come to realise that any clinging to set ways of thinking, or ways of being, may often be a defence against change: a defence against growth. What a shame to lose out on growth because of our insecurity.

In other ways too, I have come to find value in further dark times, principal of which were my five months in hospital, 2011–12, being treated for cancer. During that seemingly endless period, I was facing death as a very real possibility. Indeed I even planned my funeral. But, interestingly, I never once felt afraid.

After I had been discharged, being assured that my cancer would not return, I felt inspired to write up an account of that experience,[22] and later to put together *Learning along the Way* (Casement, 2019).

To a lesser degree, I also came to value the time when I was confined to bed after I had fallen and cracked a vertebra in 2018. It was that time of uninterrupted quiet that provided me with the stimulus to put together that last book (2019). I have thus come to believe that even the blackest of times do not have to remain unproductive.

---

[22] "My Time with Cancer" was first published on *Karnacology*, website of Karnac Books. It is now reprinted in *Learning along the Way* (2019, chapter 18).

I believe that good can emerge from even the worst experiences. But can we dare to be open to that possibility? Or might we find that we are being left too alone with unmanageable trauma?

Let us pray that we may never be left totally unsupported with what we cannot manage alone. Also, may we be similarly led to be alongside those who most need to be supported through what *they* cannot manage alone.

CHAPTER TEN

What is truth?

In putting together these early bits of writing, and my sub-sequent musings, I have found much else also.

I have come to realise that it is often through challenging 'truth,' as we have come to think of it, that we may come upon some greater truth that becomes free to surface.

In seeking to understand ourselves, or to understand others and even life itself, whenever we have *become too sure* about 'truth' any sense of 'accepted' truth can begin to ossify. Thus, whenever we regard a particular form of understanding as being 'beyond question,' something begins to die in what we thought we had understood.

So, when we begin to assume we have found ultimate truth, whatever 'truth' we are wishing to possess may begin to die within our grasp.

Where then is truth to be found?

Of course we can never find absolute truth. For, whatever we think we are finding can only be provisional, and it will always be some construction of our own thinking or of the minds of others.

Nevertheless, we can continue to look beyond our definitions of truth, those we had devised in our wish to understand whatever yet lies beyond our understanding. Then, maybe, we can become more open to the unknown, even if we can only ever see 'as through a glass darkly.'

I believe therefore that there is more freedom and richness in our not knowing than in the suffocation of some claims of sureness.

Sometimes I also think of sureness as carrying a *'curse of certainty,'* because sureness will always and inevitably lead to divisions and conflict—between differing sets of sureness. And we need look no further than the decades of death in Ireland to see what I mean.

Perhaps, therefore, we need *both* the claims of sureness, such as a priest proclaims within the faith he represents, *and* paradoxically also the non-certainty that continues to question it. For it has long been so that the priestly function has been partly to preserve the *status quo* and the prophetic function has always been to challenge it.

Maybe it is actually within that tension, between those irreconcilable positions, that we can find an aliveness in truth that is not yet entangled by the deadening that follows from any attempt at grasping it.

EPILOGUE

Two parallel journeys

In revisiting matters to do with religion I have been struck by the parallels that exist between those who seem trapped by the dogmas of theology and those who look for sureness in psychoanalysis.

In these contrasting spheres of belief we find many similarities. The disciples of each tend to adhere to those explanations of life that most appeal to them.

However, in the name of whichever group is claiming orthodoxy, and preaching whatever version of truth is being claimed as most true, we find religious groups being prepared to fight for their claims of precedence. So, throughout history, we find the world riven by wars of religion. And, at times, we find something similar can occur between rival groups in the field of psychoanalysis also.

That is why I regard religion as dangerous, especially when it is in the hands of those more preoccupied with power than in giving their lives in the service of others. And that is also why I remain wary of too much sureness in the realms of psychoanalytic practice.

By challenging set ways of thinking we can often be led towards a fresh sense of meaning. And that more individual sense of meaning can be important in our own lives also, as it will surely be important when we are with our patients.

Where then lies the Truth we may be looking for, in religion or in psychoanalysis? Can it be in the answers? Or might it more often be found in the questioning?

Namaste

May the sacred in me recognise
and salute the sacred in you

REFERENCES

Berlin, I. (1991). *The Crooked Timber of Humanity*. London: Fontana.

Bion, W. R. (1990). *Brazilian Lectures: 1973 São Paulo; 1974 Rio de Janeiro/São Paulo*. London: Karnac.

Bollas, C. (1987). *The Shadow of the Object: Psychoanalysis of the Unthought Known*. New York: Columbia University Press.

Casement, P. (1962). The Essence of Christianity, letter published in *Theology*, May: 199.

Casement, P. (1963). The paradox of unity. *Prism, 69*: 8–11.

Casement, P. (1964). A false security. *Prism, 88*: 28–30.

Casement, P. (1985). *On Learning from the Patient*. London: Routledge.

Casement, P. (1990). *Further Learning from the Patient*. London: Routledge.

Casement, P. (1994). On the wish not to know. In: V. Sinason (Ed.), *Treating Survivors of Satanist Abuse* (pp. 22–25). London: Routledge.

Casement, P. (1999). In whose image? In: S. Stein (Ed.), *Beyond Belief: Psychotherapy and Religion* (pp. 18–30). London: Karnac.

Casement, P. (2002). *Learning from Our Mistakes*. London: Routledge.

Casement, P. (2006). *Learning from Life*. London: Routledge.

Casement, P. (2018). *Ikons*—ancient and modern: looking towards the unknown. *British Journal of Psychotherapy, 34*(4): 668–672.

Casement, P. (2019). *Learning along the Way: Further Reflections on Psychoanalysis and Psychotherapy*. London: Routledge.

Dostoyevsky, F. (1879–80). *The Brothers Karamazov*. D. Magarshack (Trans.). London: Penguin Classics, 1958.

Houlden, J. L. (1992). *A Question of Identity*. London: Society for Promoting Christian Knowledge.

Houlden, J. L. (2002). *The Strange Story of the Gospels: Finding Doctrine through Narrative*. London: Society for Promoting Christian Knowledge.

Isaacs, S. (1948). The nature and function of phantasy. *International Journal of Psycho-Analysis, 29*: 73–97.

Robinson, J. A. T. (1963). *Honest to God*. London: SCM.

Williams, H. A. (1960). *God's Wisdom in Christ's Cross*. London: Mowbray.

Winnicott, D. W. (1965). *The Maturational Processes and the Facilitating Environment*. London: Hogarth.

Winnicott, D. W. (1971). *Playing and Reality*. London: Tavistock.

INDEX